Playing Up

Playing Up

Dave Hopwood

National Society/Church House Publishing
Church House, Great Smith Street, London SW1P 3NZ

National Society/Church House Publishing
Church House
Great Smith Street
London SW1P 3NZ

ISBN 0 7151 4895 8

First published in 1998 by The National Society and Church House Publishing

Cover design by Leigh Hurlock
Printed in England by the University Printing House, Cambridge

Contents

Introduction

Presenting a piece of drama is rather like telling a good story. It should capture the audience, draw them in, entertain and delight them, and leave them all the richer for having shared in the experience.

We all love a good story and the Bible is full of such things. Action, adventure, excitement, romance . . . but at times reading it can feel more like trying to figure out one of those stereograms or magic eye pictures. You stare and stare at it but never seem to be able to see things clearly . . . and although others try to help by telling you how amazing the images are, that only makes it all the more frustrating. Drama is one way to help unravel the adventures hidden in God's word. Jesus described the things of the kingdom as secrets: 'The secrets of the kingdom of heaven have been given to you . . .', and secrets often take a little detective work and perseverance.

As you journey through *Playing Up* you will find short dramatic pieces which help you to experience and pass on a few of those secrets. There are three pieces which look at the amazing Christmas story, and four more about the awful and glorious events of Easter. There are sketches on themes such as bereavement, families, telling the truth, forgiveness, talents and love, and there are pieces based directly on Biblical characters and accounts, such as the Creation, Cain and Abel, Joseph and his brothers, Ruth and Naomi, Gideon, and some of the parables. You will also encounter one or two unusual characters on your travels through these pages.

There are two pieces based on the wonderful world of the Planimals in Planimaland. And you will also bump into a couple of shady time travelling detectives known as Frisk and Dexter. And speaking of detectives, I think even the great Sherlock Holmes and Dr Watson may be found lurking between these pages.

If you are able to juggle or know anyone who can, then you should certainly feel at home with the Persistent Juggler and the Mugged Juggler; and if you prefer to tiptoe silently as you make your journey then there are one or two mimes to help you do so.

At times the background to some of these adventures may seem a little bare, but this is intentional, feel free to indulge your imagination and add your own actions and scenery, props and costumes as seems appropriate. As you tell these stories to others please bear in mind four things . . .

- **Enthusiasm** Jesus told his stories with sheer abandonment and passion! In our culture we are not used to expressing ourselves too exuberantly, but enthusiasm is contagious, and when a person is acting it does require more energy than when they are just being themselves. Acting is rather like being a Christian – it requires 100% commitment or it doesn't really work properly.

- **Honesty** These stories are based on gems, little jewels buried in the bountiful garden of God's word. But they are not always nice, straightforward or easy to understand. And they don't always have a happy ending. But we can be honest about that, and allow our audience to make of these stories what they will. God will help them to receive the pearl wrapped up in the adventure.

- **Vulnerability** St Paul wrote: 'When I am weak, then I am strong.' He put it so eloquently that I am not sure if I need say more. Rehearsals don't always go according to plan, so we often need to be prepared to be weak.

- **A huge sense of humour** I take myself far too seriously. But I hope that I take myself less seriously now than I used to! It is easy to feel that the truth should always be delivered with a stern voice and a straight face, but that may only turn people off and send them to sleep. It is important to tell these stories with a smile, there is a lot of fun in them, and after all, it was God who invented jokes, not us.

That's about it. Happy storytelling!

Dave Hopwood

Christmas

While shepherds rapped

Bible references
Luke 2.1-20

Theme
Christmas

Cast
Two shepherds (1 and 2)
Angel (A)

1 and 2 are discussing the first Christmas night while standing around a fire. They warm their hands as they speak. The angel enters later on, he is cool and should look it!

1 Brr . . . it's a chilly night for it.

2 A very, very chilly night for it. Brrrr!

(They shiver violently, shuddering and vibrating dramatically.)

1 It's so chilly – it reminds me of . . . (*Looks around and thesays ominously*) that night.

2 (*Also looks around*) That night?

1 Yep!

2 What night?

1 That night – the chilly one. When he came along.

2 Him?

1 Yep – that baby born in Bethlehem. When that huge crowd of angels nipped down here from heaven to tell us about it. They wrote a song about it ya know.

2 Did they?

(The shepherds begin clicking their fingers in a rhythm for the rap.)

1   Yes, it went something like this:

     While shepherds watched their flocks one night

     All seated on the ground,

     The Angel of the Lord came down

     And bright light shone around.

2   Say what?

1   Bright light shone around.

(Angel enters and breaks rhythm. Coolly says:)

Angel   Fear not . . .

1   *(Restart rhythm)* The angel said, for they were

     Scared out of their minds.

Angel   I've got good news – it's looking good

     For you and all mankind.

2   For us?

Angel   Yea, you and all mankind.

     For you in Bethlehem today

     A king has just popped out;

     A Saviour who is Christ the Lord,

     Get down and check it out!

1 and 2   Say what?

Angel   Get down and check it out!

     You'll find a little baby there

     In a stable made of wood,

     He'll be wrapped up in an animal trough

     And the place won't smell too good!

     Uh uh – the place won't smell too good!

1 And when the angel stopped his rap
   A million more turned up –
   All looking cool and singing strong,
   And praising God above.

   Then all them shepherds leapt on up
   And cruised into the town –
   Went round in circles trying to find out
   What was going down.

Angel They saw this stable lit up bright
   Just like a Christmas tree.
   They all rushed over, crept inside,
   And dropped on bended knee.

   The parents of the baby there –
   They looked surprised and stressed.
   The shepherds grinned, the baby stared,
   The sheep were not impressed.

1 They worshipped him – then took right off –
   Went dancing out the gate.
   Then had to tell their waiting wives
   Just why they'd come home late.

Angel All glory be to God on high
   And to the earth be peace.
   Goodwill henceforth from heaven to men
   Begin and never cease.
   Oh no, begin and never cease.

Oh no, begin and never cease.

Oh no, begin and never cease . . .

(The angel walks off still clicking his fingers as he goes.)

2   Wow! He must have been a bit special then, this baby.

1   Oh yea – he was! He had all tiny fingers – and he went goo goo, goo goo . . .

2   Yea, but I mean, he must have been different, ya know, to other babies.

1   Oh yea. Some kings came a bit later on to see him an' all. That caused a right stir.

(They click again and both say:)

1 and 2 We three kings of Orient are

One in a taxi one in a car

One on a scooter blowing his hooter

Playing a big guitar.

1   Actually they came on camels, but that doesn't rhyme with the rest of it.

2   D' you think anyone remembers the baby now?

1   Oh yea! See when he grew up he did some amazing things.

2   What? Like playing football for England?

1   No! Although he probably could have done if he had a trial for it. But he helped loads of people and he did things no one else has ever done. Yea, quite something that baby . . . Come on, I'll tell you all about it over a cup of tea. He came to be our Saviour see . . .

2   Our Saviour? What's that mean?

(They exit still talking about Jesus.)

Arfur's Christmas

Bible references
Luke 2.1-7

Theme
Christmas

Cast
Arfur, a rough and ready angel

Enter Arfur, carrying some tinsel. He sees the audience, stops and turns to them.

Arfur   Ah! There you are. Now my name's Arfur – Arfur the angel. Now I know you haven't heard of me, but we can't all be famous, can we? And I have done some pretty amazing things in my time, I promise you. Remember that story about David killing Goliath? I was there – it was my job to hand David the stone and duck. No, I don't mean I handed him a duck, I mean, I had to duck when I handed him . . . oh never mind.

Anyway, right now I'm doing a spot of time travelling. Yea, going back in time, back to Christmas. No, not last Christmas – *the* Christmas. The first one. The original. No bubble bath or Cliff Richard or Noel's House Party at this one. No, we're going to have a great time, can you imagine, we won't have to remember Christmas, we won't have to imagine how it was, we'll be there. The real thing. Listen, I'll let you into a little secret. I've got it all here, written down – on this bit of paper (*producing a scruffy bit of paper*). It's called a memo. Look, I wasn't supposed to read it yet but I'll let you hear a bit of it.

Just listen to this . . . This is what we're going to have at that first Christmas. Cobwebs, smelly animals, spiders and an old shed. Oh. Oh no, I must have got the wrong bit of paper. Drat, it's going to take me ages to get back and change it. It's miles to heaven you know, especially when you ain't got any wings yet. I have to walk it. You see I'm only on foot patrol – for the moment – but I have put in for promotion. Anyway, what am I going do about this?

(*He reads*) Camels' dung, flies, rats, hypothermia . . . sounds like a right do. Eh . . . I wonder if this is the Noah's Ark memo. Yea, that'll be it, look . . . there's a couple of pigeons, two mice, some wild dogs . . . yea. Funny – it doesn't mention any water. Plenty of noise though, and look it says a long journey in the dead of night. That'll be Noah on that boat of his. It's hardly going to be the baby Jesus in amongst all this rough stuff, is it? Can't be the birth of the King can it? If it was there'd be presents and back slapping, celebrations, hospitals, parties and an epidural. There's no mention of any of that. Ooh, hang on, it does say send along a few angels for a sing song, two million actually. Why ain't my name here? I can sing. (*He sings very badly*) 'Angels from the realms of Gloucester . . .' No that's not right. Anyway. Ooh look there is a nice soft double bed here . . . oh! Oh no – the bed's been crossed out. And so's the hotel. It just says . . . Stable. Perhaps that means The Stag and Stable? Perhaps that's the inn they're going to stay in. And the food and drink's been crossed out an' all. Doesn't sound much like Christmas to me. I'd better sort this out. I mean, Christmas is about the good things, isn't it? Hope and peace and laughter and all that. Well, where are you gonna find that in a draughty, old stable? No I gotta sort this out. I mean – there's not a word about tinsel in here, or stuffing, or the Queen's speech, or Pictionary, or huge bars of chocolate, Indiana Jones, James Bond, dear, dear, dear . . .

(*He walks off studying the list and muttering.*)

The right person for the job

Bible reference
Luke 1.26-45

Themes
Christmas; Mary; God's precise plans and timing

Cast
Two angels – 1 and 2

They are looking for the right person to be the mother of Jesus. 1 is giving 2 instructions about the person they are looking for. They walk on together and begin talking immediately. 1 has a clipboard and consults it throughout the sketch, 2 peers over 1's shoulder at the clipboard occasionally. 2 has a pen and notepad and scribbles down the details as 1 explains them.

1   Now. These are the details about the girl we're looking for. She has to be from a place called Nazareth.

2   Right. Got that.

1   But soon she must be going to a place called Bethlehem.

2   Right. And why are we looking for her?

1   She's about to receive a gift – from the Holy Spirit.

2   Oh right. The Holy Spirit. Now he has lots of gifts doesn't he? I've got a list here. (*Turns the page on his pad*) Which one is it? There's healing . . . miracles . . . prophecy . . . wisdom . . .

1   No. Pregnancy.

2   What! Are you sure? Is that one on the list?

1   Yes. I'm positive. God wants to give this person a baby. A very special baby.

2   Fair enough. Is she married?

1   No. Not yet.

2   Not yet?

1   No. But she is engaged.

2   Who to?

1   To someone who is the great grandson of King David.

2   Oh. Could you just repeat that?

1   No.

2   Fair enough. Anything else?

1   Nope. Oh yes. The person we're looking for must have a cousin.

2   A cousin?

1   Yes. Called Elizabeth.

2   Not too specific then.

1   And she has to be too old to have children.

2   Don't tell me, let me guess . . . She's gonna have a baby too, right?

1   Exactly.

2   What!! No, no . . . I was only joking . . .

1   Well, I wasn't. Now this cousin will be married to someone who won't be able to speak.

2   Why not?

1   Well, when he heard his wife was going to have a baby he was struck dumb.

2   I think I can sympathise. Anything else?

1   No, no. OH! Yes. The girl we're looking for, must be humble, brave, have a sense of humour, a lot of trust, and be ready to step into the unknown.

2   Not asking for much are we? Is that it then? Should she have blue eyes or freckles?

1   No, but she must be ready for problems, sadness, fame and rejection, and she mustn't be afraid of spiders and rats.

2   Spiders and rats? Ugh!

(2 leaps up into the arms of 1, who drops the clipboard. 2 hastily gets down again.)

Why spiders and rats?

1   Because when she gets to Bethlehem she's going to have her baby there.

2   In which hospital?

1   A shed.

2   That's a funny name for a hospital.

1   It's not a name for a hospital. It's a name for a shed. That's where the spiders and rats will be and that's where she's going to have her baby.

2   In a shed!

1   Yes. Well, that's about it. Any more questions?

2   Just one. Have you been looking for this person for long?

1   Oh yes. Months.

2   Months?

1   Well . . . years.

2   Years?

1   Yes. Years . . . and years . . . and years . . . and years. Decades actually. Centuries. For hundreds of years we've sent out the spies looking for the right girl to be the mother of God's baby. And every generation so far we've drawn a blank. We haven't found the right person.

2   Perhaps you're being a bit too specific. I mean, why don't we just try to find someone with brown hair, blue eyes and a pet hamster.

1   No!

2   No?

1   No. Of course not. (*Jabs the clipboard.*) All these details are very important. It is vital we find exactly the right person for this job. And we know we'll find her one day. We know she'll be out there. When the time's exactly right. Okay, it's time to start looking again. This is the latest news – we've heard about a young girl in a place called Galilee, I think you should try there. Her name's . . .

(*He moves the clipboard closer and further away, as if trying to read his own writing.*)

Her name's Mmm . . . (*Pause.*)

2   Martha?

1   No.

2   Maggie?

1   No.

2   Mathilda?

1   No.

2   Mary?

1   No. Yes! That's it. Brilliant. Mary – her name's Mary. That's the one. Go get her Gabriel!

(*Both exit in a hurry.*)

Note on Planimaland

The following two sketches take place in Planimaland. They should be presented by a group of children, who are each allocated an animal to represent in the story. When they each hear their respective animal mentioned they stand up or step forward and do the appropriate action. There are some actions which everyone should do, and you may like to add other animals, actions or sounds of your own choosing. You might also like to add costumes, make up or masks, or even make puppets to represent the different characters in the story. Alternatively, you may like to teach responses to the whole audience or congregation, and then everyone can join in with the story. To do this you may like to get a group to lead the responses from the front, or one person may simply narrate the story to the audience after teaching them the responses. The responses are fairly simple and repetitive so that young children can be involved in telling the stories. Each story begins with the same introductory paragraph which may be omitted if your audience is familiar with the characters.

Christmas with the Planimals

Bible references
Luke 1.26-38 and Luke 2.1-20

Theme
Christmas

Cast
Narrator
Dog Rose
Pussy Willow
Goose Grass
Dandy Lion
Tiger Lily
Monkey Puzzle

Narrator Welcome to Planimaland. The place where the planimals live. There's Dog Rose . . .

(Dog Rose stands up and barks and pants.)

And Pussy Willow . . .

(Pussy Willow stands up and miaows and washes her face.)

And Goose Grass

(Goose Grass stands up and says: 'Honk, honk!')

And Spider Plant

(Every one runs their fingers over each other.)

And Dandy Lion

(*Dandy Lion stands up and roars in a rather posh and lazy way.*)

> And Tiger Lily

(*Tiger Lily roars more ferociously and everyone jumps.*)

> And of course, Monkey Puzzle.

(*Monkey Puzzle stands up and says: 'Ooh ooh, ahh ahh!' and scratches armpits.*)

> Now one day, on Christmas eve, Dandy Lion

(*Dandy Lion stands up and roars in a rather posh and lazy way.*)

> Invited all the planimals around to his house for mince pies

(*All the planimals make their noises.*)

> And so they could hear again the story of how Christmas started. Monkey Puzzle

(*Monkey Puzzle stands up and says: 'Ooh ooh, ahh ahh!' and scratches armpits.*)

> Brought some loud crackers.

(*All pretend to pull crackers and say: 'Bang!'*)

> Tiger Lily

(*Tiger Lily roars more ferociously and everyone jumps.*)

> Brought some crinkly streamers

(*All say: 'Crinkle crinkle!' and pretend to wave streamers.*)

> Goose Grass

(*Goose Grass stands up and says: 'Honk, honk!'*)

> Brought some Christmas songs

(*All sing: 'Jingle bells, jingle bells . . .'*)

> And Dog Rose and Pussy Willow

(*Dog Rose stands up and barks and pants. Pussy Willow stands up and miaows and washes her face.*)

> Brought some presents for everyone.

(*All say: 'Ooooh!'*)

> They all sat round the big Christmas tree and Dandy Lion started.

15

(*Dandy Lion stands up and roars in a rather posh and lazy way.*)

> Once there was a young woman called Mary, and she saw an angel.

(*All smile and flap wings like an angel.*)

> The angel said to her: 'Don't be afraid!

(*All look scared.*)

> You're going to have a beautiful baby.

(*All hold baby in arms.*)

> He's going to be a boy and God wants you to call him Jesus.'

> The next bit of the story was told by Tiger Lily.

(*Tiger Lily roars more ferociously and everyone jumps.*)

> Mary was going to be married to a man called Joseph. And he saw the angel too.

(*All smile and flap wings like an angel.*)

> He saw it in a dream while he was asleep.

(*All snore loudly.*)

> And the angel told him not to be afraid.

(*All look scared.*)

> And the angel told him about the baby.

(*All hold baby in arms.*)

> The next bit of the story was told by Goose Grass.

(*Goose Grass stands up and says: 'Honk, honk!'*)

> Just before the baby was born Mary and Joseph had to go to a place called Bethlehem.

(*All sing: 'Oh little town of Bethlehem . . .'*)

> When they got there the town was full of people and it was a bit of a squash.

(*All squeeze together and look squashed.*)

All the hotels and guest houses were full. The only place they could stay in was an old cow shed.

(*All say: 'Mooooo!'*)

So they went in there and that was where Mary had her baby.

(*All hold baby in arms.*)

She wrapped him in bits of cloth and they used the cow's food trough as a cot.

(*Pretend to lower baby gently into an imaginary cot.*)

They called the baby Jesus and lots of people came to see him because they knew he was someone very special.

(*All clap their hands.*)

That was the end of their Christmas story so Tiger Lily

(*Tiger Lily roars more ferociously and everyone jumps.*)

Dandy Lion, Pussy Willow, Dog Rose, Monkey Puzzle and Goose Grass

(*All make their noises as their name is called out.*)

All curled up by the Christmas tree and fell fast asleep.

(*All curl up and sleep and snore.*)

Easter

Easter in Planimaland

Theme
Easter

Cast
Narrator
Dog Rose
Pussy Willow
Goose Grass
Dandy Lion
Tiger Lily
Monkey Puzzle

Narrator   Welcome to Planimaland. The place where the planimals live.
There's Dog Rose . . .

(*Dog Rose stands up and barks and pants.*)

And Pussy Willow . . .

(*Pussy Willow stands up and miaows and washes her face.*)

And Goose Grass

(*Goose Grass stands up and says: 'Honk, honk!'*)

And Spider Plant

(*Every one runs their fingers over each other.*)

And Dandy Lion

(*Dandy Lion stands up and roars in a rather posh and lazy way.*)

And Tiger Lily

(*Tiger Lily roars more ferociously and everyone jumps.*)

And of course, Monkey Puzzle.

(Monkey Puzzle stands up and says: 'Ooh ooh, ahh ahh!' and scratches armpits.)

Now one day Dog Rose

(Dog Rose stands up and barks and pants.)

Was taking a quiet snooze in the garden.

(All pretend to sleep.)

The birds were tweeting

(All make bird noises.)

The bees were buzzing

(All make buzzing bee noises.)

And a gentle breeze was blowing around the flowers and trees.

(All make the sound of the wind whistling around.)

Suddenly

(All look up shocked.)

Pussy Willow came bounding up the garden.

(Pussy Willow stands up and miaows and washes her face.)

'It's time for the great Easter egg hunt,' she said. And all the other planimals ran in from nowhere.

(All the planimals make their noises.)

So Dog Rose woke up

(Dog Rose stands up and barks and pants.)

And the search for the Easter eggs began. They all hunted high

(They all look up high.)

And low

(They all look down at the ground.)

They looked in each other's pockets

(They do this.)

And they looked in each other's mouths.

But no one found the Easter eggs.

'They're not here', said Tiger Lily.

(*Tiger Lily roars ferociously and everyone jumps.*)

'But they must be here – it's Easter!' said Dandy Lion.

(*Dandy Lion stands up and roars in a rather posh and lazy way.*)

'It won't be Easter without the eggs', said Goose Grass.

(*Goose Grass stands up and says: 'Honk, honk!'*)

But then Monkey Puzzle stood up.

(*Monkey Puzzle stands up and says: 'Ooh ooh, ahh ahh!' and scratches armpits.*)

'I know a story about Easter', he said. 'There was a once a man who had lots of friends.

(*All huddle together as a big group of friends.*)

Lots of people liked him and people came from everywhere to meet him.

(*They all shake hands with each other.*)

But one day, there was a man who didn't like him

(*All growl at the audience.*)

And he persuaded everyone to get rid of the man and his friends.

(*All look sad.*)

So they killed him and all his friends ran away.

(*Run on the spot.*)

Suddenly

(*All look shocked.*)

Three days later – the man came back to life again. He was perfectly okay and everyone was amazed.'

(*All cheer.*)

'I've found the Easter eggs', said Dandy Lion.

(*Dandy Lion stands up and roars in a rather posh and lazy way.*)

They were in a big bag, and no one had remembered to hide them for the big Easter egg hunt.

(*All put hand to head and shake heads and then shrug.*)

'No wonder we couldn't find them', said Goose Grass.

(*Goose Grass stands up and says: 'Honk, honk!'*)

And so they all had an Easter egg and they tasted delicious.

(*All mime chewing and say: 'Mmmmmmm!'*)

The ingredients of the first Easter

Bible references
Luke 23.13-34

Themes
Easter; Jesus taking our place, dying so we might live

Cast
Narrator

Four who begin as one group, doing the same actions together, then become four characters:

Two guards

Judge

Prisoner

A fifth actor, playing the part of Jesus, sits in the front row of the audience until pulled out by the guards

Narrator At Easter we have eggs.

(*The group make chicken sounds and strut around the stage.*)

Not those sort of eggs – chocolate ones.

(*They all mime eating noisily with their mouths full.*)

And we have hot cross buns

(*Blow on fingers and try to eat a hot bun with difficulty.*)

And Easter bunnies.

(*All hop and stick teeth out, looking like bunnies.*)

But it wasn't always like that.

(*At this point the four become the different characters.*)

These were the ingredients of the first Easter. There were huge ugly soldiers.

(*Two of the group become menacing soldiers, pulling ugly faces and strutting about the stage, threatening the audience.*)

There was a very naughty criminal.

(*The two guards mime chewing gum and stand feet apart, arms folded, looking menacing. A third member of the group becomes the criminal prisoner. He looks shifty, tip toes across the stage and creeps up on the fourth member of the group who is now miming reading a newspaper. The prisoner picks his pocket so that the audience can see this but not the person reading the paper.*)

And he was arrested.

(*'You're nicked!' The two guards say this as they grab the prisoner and each place a heavy hand on one of his shoulders, holding him between them. The prisoner leaps up in fright as they do this. If the guards are strong enough they might like to lift the prisoner off the floor by the arms. The prisoner looks horrified.*)

Then there was a judge.

(*The fourth member of the group becomes the judge, mimes placing a wig on his head, adopts a stoop and studies the prisoner closely.*)

And there was a trial.

(*The guards turn the prisoner to face the judge. The judge punches his palm, points at the prisoner and says: 'You're guilty, young man'.*)

And the man was thrown into prison.

(*The guards push the prisoner into a prison and mime shutting the door. They all say a loud 'Clang!' as the door slams shut. The prisoner mimes holding the bars and the guards throw bits of food inside saying: 'Bread', 'Water', 'Bread', 'Water', 'Bread', 'Water', 'Bread', 'Water'. The prisoner interrupts and says: 'I can't believe there's no butter!' The guards stop, look at him and say 'Shut up!' And they resume their 'Bread', 'Water' routine.*)

And finally he was executed in a horrible way.

(*They pull the prisoner forward, stretch out his arms and mime pulling hammers and nails from their pockets. They are about to nail him up, with the nails pressed into his palms, and their arms stretched back about to hammer when they freeze as the narrator says:*)

Stop! Now at this point we'll freeze the picture. Because that isn't the way it happened. Take him down.

(The guards protest. 'Oh!' 'But why?' 'That's not fair!' 'I was just enjoying myself!')

Take him down!

(They release him, the prisoner looks ecstatic. He leaps in the air and runs madly round in circles. The guards say: 'What's wrong? Is he innocent then?')

Oh no, not all, he was very guilty.

(The guards say: 'Good!' and grab the prisoner again. The prisoner looks crest-fallen.)

The man's name was Barabbas and he was a nasty, smelly, despicable, horrible character.

(Barabbas leers at the audience and the guards smell his armpits and recoil at the stench. They both faint from the smell.)

And he certainly was guilty of lots of crimes.

(Barabbas says 'Shhh!' and tries to hush the narrator. He begins to tiptoe off stage but the soldiers wake up, leap up and grab him again and start to nail him onto the cross again.)

But there was no way he was going to be executed. So they let him go.

(Barabbas runs off leaping and laughing. He exits, cheering off stage as he goes.)

And they did this because a different man was arrested and charged and killed in his place.

(The guards pull a person out of the audience, a fifth actor who had slipped in earlier, and hold him up and mime nailing him to the cross. They freeze this picture, and then the narrator continues:)

This man's name was Jesus Christ, and he not only died so that Barabbas could live, he died so that we could live too. He died in our place, because he loved us so much.

(All kneel at the feet of the crucified Jesus. Hold this final picture, the narrator kneeling too.)

Easter group mime

Bible references
Luke 19.37-40; Luke 20.47-23, 49; Luke 24.1-12

Themes
The events of Palm Sunday, Good Friday and Easter Sunday

Cast
Jesus

Peter

Pilate

An ensemble cast of ten or more who play the parts
of the crowd, the pharisees, the disciples, the guards

This is a group mime which relies upon the whole cast to make it effective. It requires some background music and you may like to choose your own for this. You may choose one piece of music for the entire piece or three different pieces, one for each part. This piece may be used effectively outside or inside, and it may be performed by adults or children, or a mixed group. The beauty of a piece like this is that it allows the group to input their own characters and ideas, and the piece will vary depending on those performing it. The stage directions here are the bones of the piece; feel free to add extra characters and incidents as you feel appropriate. This is also a good workshop exercise, and doesn't have to be a performance piece. Your group may get a lot from simply experiencing the story of Easter afresh as they put this piece together.

Part 1: Palm Sunday (*Music should be of a lively nature.*)
The scene is a town centre. Begin with people frozen in positions of sleeping, talking, shopping, laughing, eating etc. As the music begins they start to move and do these things. Then Jesus enters with Peter,

they mime having a conversation. Jesus stops to write in the sand and Peter stoops down alongside him. They discuss what Jesus has written. One by one the people spot Jesus and start to come over. Jesus gets up and goes to meet them, they throng around him, some touching, some shaking hands, patting him, pointing, reminding him of ways he has helped and healed some of them. They all move slowly to centre stage rear, still talking excitedly and with Jesus in the midst of them. Then they bring on a chair, or a box, or a stepladder and lift him up and stand him on it and then they all freeze with their hands stretching up and reaching out to him.

Part 2: Good Friday (*Music should be dark, sombre and menacing.*)
Their reaching hands change to angry fists and as some of them grab Jesus by the clothes and pull him down, all the crowd's fists move as one in the same pulling down motion. Jesus is left lying on the floor in the dust as the crowd disperses and moves away. Two of the crowd become guards who pull Jesus to his feet and push him to centre stage front, and there they stand either side of him and hold his arms and wrists out and to the side. Peter hangs back and watches from a distance. The crowd forms two lines of pharisees and the scene is now the trial. They sit or stand behind Jesus, facing each other in two parallel lines running from stage front to stage rear. Pilate steps forward and circles Jesus, staring him in the face all the time, and as he does so the crowd slowly lifts up accusing fingers, pointing them straight at Jesus. Pilate completes the circle, raises his own finger, pauses, then changes it to an upraised thumb. He then slowly turns his thumb down and the crowd follows this and does the same. He snaps his fingers and beckons to two of the pharisees, who step forward and stand facing each other each side of and directly behind Jesus. Pilate then steps away and washes his hands, while the guards drape Jesus over the shoulders of the two pharisees in a broken crucifixion position. (N.B. the two people forming the cross should be about the same height as the person playing Jesus.) Peter, who has remained at the rear of the stage until now, moves forward at this point to try and help but as everyone turns to look at him he backs away, looks terrified and buries his head in his

hands. The guards then step away to stage right and left of Jesus and they stand callously chewing and leaning on spears while the rest of the cast walks around Jesus, each one pausing for a moment to look, spit, kneel, cry, laugh, shake heads, accuse, etc. (Whatever each person feels their character would do.) They then return to their seats one by one and gradually fall asleep. The guards step back in and stand in front of Jesus, slightly apart, so that the audience can still see Jesus. Pilate stands off with his back to Jesus.

Part 3: Easter Sunday (*Music should begin softly then build to a lively climax.*)

Jesus begins to come back to life, first by merely flicking one of his fingers, then another and another. Then he begins twitching his hands and his arms and he begins lifting and dropping his chest as if gasping for breath. He keeps his eyes closed and head bowed while he does this. Try not to rush this sequence of events. Eventually he brings his head up sharply and his eyes burst open. He pulls one arm then the other arm off the cross, breaking free from the cross, and he then stretches, massages his wrists, rubs his face and wakes up fully. He then steps forward and sits cross legged at the front of the stage. He thinks, looks up into the sky and then begins writing in the sand. Meanwhile the guards and the two people forming the cross have seen this and they have scarpered, running around to wake the others one by one. As they begin to see Jesus, risen and alive, they each make their own response, some running, some creeping forward, some holding back, some scared, some unsure, some shunning him. Freeze with this closing picture, some of the people around or approaching Jesus, some hanging back, some hesitant, some with their backs turned. (*Music fades or finishes.*)

Mr X

Bible references
Luke 20.9-18

Themes
The parable of the workers in the vineyard; the Easter story

Cast
Narrator

A group of four who mime to the narrative

Begin with the group of four frozen, the rich man counting his money and the others waiting on him.

Narrator There was once a rich man called Mr X

(One stands upright and counts money, others polish his shoes and dust him down.)

Who owned a twelve screen cinema multiplex,

(Look up in wonder and amazement.)

With all the latest movies and take away food,

(Pretend to sit watching an imaginary film.)

American ice cream and pop corn too.

(Stuff popcorn into mouth while watching.)

He rented out the place to a group of friends

(All bunch together like a group of old friends.)

Who wanted the place for a whole weekend.

(Rub hands excitedly.)

For forty-eight hours they sat in the dark

(All look dazed and spaced out.)

Watching James Bond, Batman and Jurassic Park.

(*Pose as James Bond, Batman or a dinosaur.*)

But the friends decided they wanted to stay

(*Stand defiantly with arms crossed.*)

They liked it so much they wouldn't go away.

(*Hold up hands and shake heads.*)

They drank all the coke and ate all the sweets

(*Pick up a huge carton of coke and drink it down.*)

And left chewing gum splattered over all of the seats.

(*Chew gum and stretch it out of mouth with fingers.*)

So the rich man sent his chauffeur along,

(*One of group drive a car, others look at him.*)

To ask them if they planned on staying long.

(*All tap watch and check that it's working.*)

But when they saw him coming they hatched a plan.

(*Chauffeur drives. Others form a circle as if plotting something secretly.*)

Took some hot fudge sauce and threw it over the man.

(*The group turn and mime throwing buckets of sauce. The chauffeur freezes and clamps his eyes shut as if hit by the sauce.*)

The rich man's accountant was a real mean dude,

(*The same member of the group who played the chauffeur now becomes the accountant and mimes tapping on a calculator, others look at him.*)

He came with a bill for the films and the food.

(*All count on fingers and look shocked at the number.*)

They waited on the roof and when he knocked on the doors

(*Half of the group jump on the backs of the other half.*)

They sprayed him with mustard and hot dog sauce.

(When accountant knocks on an imaginary door, those on the backs of the others mime spraying him. The accountant shields himself and looks shocked.)

So the rich man sent his bodyguard round

(The accountant now becomes the bodyguard, flexing muscles and looking mean. Others watch.)

To sort out the trouble that was going down.

(The bodyguard turns and threatens the group who all cower and look terrified.)

They showed him the saddest film they could find

(The bodyguard watches film and starts to cry.)

And while he was crying they crept up from behind.

(They creep up and bop him on the head. The bodyguard falls to the floor.)

So Mr X had a good long think,

(All adopt thinking poses.)

Things were going bad and starting to stink.

(All hold noses and pull faces.)

He reckoned it was time to send his boy

(The person who has played the part of the chauffeur, accountant and bodyguard now becomes the son, and they all point to him.)

He knew they'd listen to his pride and joy.

(All lean towards the son and place a hand to their ear, listening as the son mimes talking.)

When they saw the son they were over the moon.

(They look ecstatic.)

'Let's kill him!' they said, 'and let's do it soon'.

(They each draw a finger across their throats.)

So they ambushed him and they laid a trap

(They grab the son.)

Then they dragged him to the car park around the back.

Playing Up

(*They pick him up between them and walk in a circle.*)

They strung up the boy and they left him alone.
(*They put him into a crucifixion pose.*)

Left him on the cross till his life was gone.
(*The boy bows his head and dies.*)

After six long hours they took him down,
(*They take down the body.*)

Then they buried him in a big hole in the ground.
(*They lay him on the floor behind them.*)

Then they went to watch a Disney film in screen one
(*They watch film in a line and eat popcorn.*)

And while they were watching something strange went on.
(*They frown and look all around and start to shake.*)

The ground began to shake and they fell on the floor
(*They continue to shake and shiver and fall down.*)

When they got back up there was a knock at the door.
(*They stand up and listen.*)

With trembling hands they turned the key,
(*They reach out to stage front.*)

And standing there for them all to see
(*They look shocked, and stare open mouthed.*)

Was Mr X, he'd been there a while
(*They back away.*)

He didn't look happy and he didn't smile.
(*They drop to their knees.*)

Mr X made them stand in line

(They all leap forward as if pushed.)

And he took them for a walk to the scene of the crime.

(They step forward and freeze. Behind them the son gets up and steps stage left.)

Then he pointed to the place where they'd buried his son

(They turn and look behind them.)

But the hole was empty and the son had gone.

(They gather round and look at the spot where the son was.)

When they turned back round they got a shock right then

(The boy taps one of them on the shoulder.)

'Cause the boy was alive he'd come back again.

(They look, jump and some of them faint into the arms of the others.)

'I've come for my boy', the rich man said.

(They gather round the boy and look at his hands and body.)

'I came to find him and bring him back from the dead.'

(They drop down at the son's feet, some hold head in hands, some look up.)

The Ten Commandments

The case of the golden calf

Bible references
Exodus 19, 20 and 32

Themes
The ten commandments; worshipping God

Cast
Narrator
Sherlock Holmes
Dr Watson

Narrator Imagine a huge mountain.

(*Holmes and Watson walk on, look up, point and shield their eyes.*)

Imagine a thick cloud all around.

(*They try and sweep the mist away with their hands.*)

And the sound of distant thunder.

(*They place a hand to their ears and listen and quite obviously make the noise themselves.*)

Then add some smoke on the mountain

(*They both cough like mad.*)

And you have the strange case of the golden calf. Now, over to the world famous detectives – Sherlock Holmes and Dr Watson.

Watson (*Watson points and says:*)

I say Holmes look! A mountain.

Holmes Very astute Watson, but what do you make of these?

(*Holmes points at the floor.*)

Watson	Correct me if I'm wrong, but they look like your shoes. And awfully nice they are too.
Holmes	No, Watson, use your imagination. I'm talking about these bits of stone.
Narrator	And Holmes picked up the bits of stone.
	(*He mimes this.*)
Narrator	And Dr Watson said 'Hmmm'.
Watson	Hmmm.
Narrator	Then Holmes turned round and his mouth fell open.

(*Holmes turns stage right and open his mouth wide.*)

Then Watson turned round and his mouth fell open.

(*Watson does the same.*)

Narrator	There in front of them was a huge golden calf.
Watson	I say Holmes, what's this all about?
Narrator	Asked Watson. Holmes pointed at the ground. There were thousands of footprints in the sand all around them.
Holmes	There's been rather a lot of people here.
Narrator	He said, and he picked up an empty cup and smelt it.

(*Holmes sniffs loudly.*)

Holmes	And they had a party. Looks like an open and shut case to me.
Watson	I say Holmes, that's clever of you. Can we go home then and have a nice cup of tea?
Holmes	Aren't you suppose to say, tell me what you've deduced?
Watson	I don't know Holmes. Am I?
Holmes	Yes, but I'll tell you anyway.
Narrator	Holmes pointed at the stones.
Holmes	Watson, those are the ten commandments.
Narrator	He said.
Holmes	Shh! That mountain is called Mount Sinai. Moses, my dear Watson, went up there to meet with God. And that was where

God gave him the ten commandments, carved on two slabs of stone. But while he was gone, I'm sorry to inform you, the people built this. The golden calf.

Watson   But why Holmes, surely they couldn't eat it!

Narrator   Holmes laughed.

Holmes   Ha, ha, ha. Well done Watson. They certainly couldn't. But they could bow down and worship it.

Watson   Seems jolly silly Holmes.

Holmes   And so it is Watson. That's why Moses broke the stones when he saw the calf. Because while Moses was talking to God, the people had given up and decided to worship this calf instead. And one of the commandments clearly states that one shouldn't worship anything but God.

Watson   I say Holmes you are jolly clever. What are all these ten commandments?

Holmes   Rules for living Watson. Rules for living. Don't steal, don't lie, don't swear, don't kill . . .

Watson   I say! If people stuck to those we'd be out of a job Holmes.

Holmes   Hmm, I do believe you're right Watson. Now that's a sobering thought.

Narrator   And they went back to 221b Baker Street for a nice cup of tea.

(*They wander off.*)

Watson   I say Holmes those are awfully nice shoes you're wearing, I don't suppose I could borrow them sometime?

Friendship and family

The mugged juggler

Bible references
Luke 10.25-37

Theme
The Good Samaritan

Cast
Juggler
Two muggers
Tennis player
Snooker player
Shopper

Begin with the juggler juggling on stage. The two muggers run on and push him over and grab the juggling balls and run off. The juggler gets up and rubs his bruises, he looks bored and miserable and kicks the ground. Enter the tennis player, carrying a racket and three balls.

Juggler	Hey! Can I borrow those tennis balls?
Tennis player	Why?
Juggler	To juggle with. Some people stole my juggling balls and now I'm lost without them.
Tennis player	Well, tough, I've got a match to play.

(Tennis player storms off muttering. Juggler looks fed up and disappointed. He sighs. Enter the snooker player, carrying a cue and some snooker balls.)

Juggler	Hey! Can I borrow your snooker balls.
Snooker player	*(Suspicious)* Why?
Juggler	For juggling.

Snooker player   You can't juggle with snooker balls!

Juggler   Oh yes I can!

Snooker player   Oh no you can't!

Juggler   Oh yes I can!

Snooker player   Prove it.

(He hands over three balls. Juggler takes them and eagerly begins juggling with them.)

Juggler   See!

Snooker player   Hmmm! Well, you still can't have 'em!

(And the snooker player grabs them and walks off, leaving the juggler sad again. Enter the shopper with a bag full of stuff. He stops when he sees the juggler.)

Shopper   Are you all right?

(The juggler shakes his head sadly).

Shopper   What's wrong?

Juggler   I love juggling, but no one will help me out. I was robbed and I don't have anything to juggle with now.

Shopper   Oh! Well, I don't have any juggling balls but . . .

Shopper begins to look through bag.

Shopper   How about these? Will they do?

(He brings out three items – whatever you choose for the sketch. The juggler's face lights up, he takes them and begins juggling. The shopper applauds.)

Juggler   Hey! Thanks! This is great!

(They walk off together, happily juggling and talking.)

The banana party

Bible references
Luke 14.15-24

Themes
The Good Samaritan

Cast
One
Two
Three
Four
Five

Props
One dry weetabix
One can of cream
One Mars Bar
Bag of balloons
Bag of marshmallows
One banana

One   Right. Have we got the weetabix?

(*Two takes a bite out of the weetabix.*)

    The squirty cream?

(*Three squirts some cream and eats it.*)

    The Mars bars?

(*Four takes a bite of Mars bar.*)

    The balloons?

(*Two blows up a balloon and lets it down again.*)

The marshmallows?

(*Three has a marshmallow.*)

The bananas?

(*Four has a bite of banana.*)

Okay we're all set for the banana party then. I love bananas it's going to be . . . Oh! Is that the time? Sorry I've got to go. I've got to watch 'Neighbours'.

Two   (*Picks up list.*)

Okay, let's double check.

Right   Have we got the weetabix?

(*Four takes a bite out of the weetabix.*)

The squirty cream?

(*Three squirts some cream and eats it.*)

The Mars bars?

(*Four takes a bite of Mars bar.*)

The balloons?

(*Four blows up the balloon.*)

The marshmallows?

(*Three eats a marshmallow.*)

The bananas?

(*Four has a bite of banana.*)

Great! Oh! Is that the time? I've got to go shopping.

Three   (*Picks up list.*)

Right. Let's triple check.

Have we got the weetabix?

The squirty cream?

The Mars bars?

The balloons?

The marshmallows?

The bananas?

(*Four eats all of these.*)

Good. I'm off then. I've got to go to tennis practice.

Five   Hey you look like you were having fun!

Four   Yea, it was supposed to be a banana party for all my family and friends.

Five   Well you've got the bananas. Where's the family and friends?

Four   They had other things to do.

Five   Oh. Tell you what. I know lots of people who'd love a party.

Four   Really?

Five   Yea, and they love bananas and dry weetabix. Shall we go and invite them instead?

(*They exit.*)

Cain and Abel

Bible references
Genesis 4

Themes
Harvest; God's provision; jealousy; family

Cast
Narrator
Cain
Abel

Begin with the narrator alone on stage.

Narrator   Welcome to the story of Cain and Abel. This is a story about brothers, about families, about harvest and farmers, about sheep and lambs. Sounds a nice story doesn't it? Let's see what happens . . .

(Enter Cain and Abel. They see the audience and wave and step forward as they speak.)

Cain   Hello. My name's Cain.

Abel   And my name's Abel.

Cain   Abel is my brother.

Abel   And Cain is my brother.

Cain   I'm a farmer.

Abel   And I'm a shepherd.

Cain   And this is how we do our work.

(They mime their work. Cain sows seeds and pulls up weeds. Abel calls to the sheep and whistles at them. He picks up a large one and carries it.)

Narrator   Cain is a farmer, he goes out into the fields and sows lots of crops like wheat and corn. He hopes to make weetabix and cornflakes and sell them at a big profit! Abel is a shepherd, that means he looks after lots of sheep. He's good at his job and takes care of them very well.

Cain   Soon it'll be harvest time.

Abel   Soon it'll be lambing time.

Narrator   Baaaaaaa! Baaaa . . .

(*Cain and Abel look at the narrator, who gives an apologetic shrug and then smiles. Cain mimes cutting the harvest with a sickle. Abel picks up a little lamb and strokes it.*)

Cain   It's a satisfying feeling to see what you've grown.

Abel   Just look at all these lambs. They're lovely. God's certainly blessed my work.

Cain   (*Looking up*) God? Oh yes. Of course. I mustn't forget him, I suppose. Without God I er . . . don't suppose I would have anything. Yes, probably not . . . I wonder how much I can sell all this weetabix for?

(*He looks at an imaginary pile of boxes.*)

Cain   I think I'd better give some of these to God to say a little thank-you for this really good harvest.

(*He picks up one or two of the boxes, then changes his mind and grabs a few little bits of straw from the floor. Abel picks up a lamb and holds it up.*)

Abel   My prize lamb. Thank you God for all you've given me.

(*Cain watches him, looking a bit fed up.*)

Cain   Hmm. He has got a lot of sheep. Wonder if I can have some. (*Looks up*) Oh. Thanks Lord, I've brought you one or two odd bits and pieces from my harvest.

(*He holds them up half-heartedly then forgets them, leaves them on the ground and hurries over to Abel.*)

Cain   Hi Abel, how's it going? You've got a lot of sheep. Can I have that one?

(*Cain points at one of them.*)

Abel   No you can't.

(*Abel mimes stroking the sheep and feeding them.*)

Cain Oh! But that's not fair. You've got millions.

Abel Yes, but that's not the point.

Cain You're mean you are. You always think you're better than me. Just because you're the youngest you always got spoilt. Why can't I have that lamb?

Abel Because you can't. (*He continues feeding his sheep.*)

Cain Why not?

Abel Because that's the one I've given to God.

Cain Well . . . Tell you what – you could have the stuff I've given to God in exchange for your lamb. I'm sure God wouldn't mind. He won't miss it.

Abel I'm sure he won't! That pile of old weeds! Who'd want that? Look at it. You've given God all the scraps and leftovers.

(*Cain walks over and looks at his imaginary offering then he mutters to himself and walks back. Abel is stroking one of his sheep.*)

Cain Abel?

Abel Yes?

Cain Look over there.

(*Abel looks offstage and Cain bashes him over the head with his hand. Abel falls to the ground. Cain looks at him then steps over the body.*)

Cain Hello. My name's Cain. I used to have a brother called Abel. But not any more. I think I got a bit jealous and he got a bit dead. Goodbye.

(*Cain turns and walk offstage.*)

Narrator So Cain killed his brother Abel, and our story didn't have a happy end after all. Sometimes we look at what other people have instead of looking at all the things that we have ourselves, and that can make us jealous. So don't forget about Cain and Abel, and what happened to them.

(*Narrator picks up a lamb, strokes it and says:*)

Narrator Baaaaa! (*He waves at the audience*) Goodbye everybody!

(*Narrator exits.*)

Times of work, rest and play

The Flying Scotsman

Bible references
Exodus 20.8-11

Themes
The story of Eric Liddell, his dedication to God and his desire to respect Sunday as a different day set aside for worship

Cast
A reporter armed with a microphone
Two runners

The two runners walk on in slow motion to the theme music from Chariots of Fire by Vangelis. They crouch down, mime digging out holes for starting positions with trowels, place feet in imaginary holes, take position and look up. Freeze. The reporter walks on.

Reporter Good morning ladies and gentlemen, boys and girls and welcome to the 1924 Paris Olympics. It's a fine day here at the moment and we're about to witness the final of the men's 400 metre race. But before we do that . . .

(The runners collapse.)

Oh! Sorry, er . . . yes. Have a rest. In fact, let's go back to the beginning of the story. Back to the Highlands of Scotland, back to a man in training for the race of his life.

(The runners do exercises, sit ups, star jumps, press ups, finger exercises, then perhaps finish with a clapping game.)

Eric Liddell was a rugby player.

(One of the two tackles the other.)

He was also a student.

Playing Up

(*Read books very fast.*)

And he was a sprinter.

(*Freeze in running positions.*)

In those days they had yards instead of metres.

(*Scratch heads. Measure each other with tape measures etc.*)

And instead of starting blocks, they used to dig a hole in the track for their feet.

(*They both mime digging with spades.*)

Er – but they only used little trowels.

(*They throw their spades away and look embarrassed and try and push the sand back into the holes quickly with their hands and feet.*)

And Eric Liddell won races in the 100 yards, 200 yards and 440 yards.

(*One puts medal on the other and mimes clapping.*)

In one amazing race in 1923, he was pushed over and fell just after the start.

(*One pushes the other who falls looking dismayed.*)

It was all over. He had no chance of winning.

(*The fallen runner shakes his head and looks down, while the other runner runs on in slow motion.*)

But suddenly – he got up, caught up with all the others and still won the race.

(*The fallen runner leaps up and races past the other one who looks amazed.*)

He was one of the finest runners of his time.

(*The loser pats him on the back.*)

And so we come to the 1924 Olympic games in Paris. And the 100 yards final.

(*They go back to miming in slow motion and dig the holes again.*)

The race to be the fastest man in the world.

(*Then they adopt the starting position.*)

The athletes took their positions, placed their feet in the holes, looked down the track and waited for the starting pistol.

(*They freeze about to start. The reporter mimes holding up a starting pistol.*)

However. Eric Liddell wasn't there.

(*They look horrified and collapse again.*)

He wanted to be there and he could have won.

(*They take up their positions again. The reporter holds up the starting pistol again.*)

But he wasn't.

(*They give up and collapse.*)

And he had a very good reason.

(*The reporter beckons to the two runners who come close to the reporter and listen.*)

Eric Liddell was a Christian. And on Sunday he went to church and he worshipped God.

(*The runners look surprised.*)

And on a Sunday he wouldn't run in any races because he wanted to make it a different day, set aside for God.

(*One of the runners prays, the other reads the Bible.*)

And the races for the Olympic 100 yards were on a Sunday. So in spite of really wanting to run,

(*The runners look really excited.*)

He wouldn't do it. Because God was the most important thing in Eric Liddell's life.

(*The runners shake their heads and start walking off stage.*)

So instead – he ran in the 440 yards final.

(*The runners look back, realise and hurriedly take up their positions again.*)

And . . . he won.

(*They run in slow motion and one wins the race.*)

Because God had made him very fast.

(*All freeze looking up.*)

Seven days

Bible references

Genesis 1 and Exodus 20.8-11

Themes

Creation; relationship between man and God and the importance of a
day of rest

Cast

Father

Son

*The Father opens a large book and places it on a table. The Father and Son look
at it.*

Father Right now Son, these are the blueprints of the plans for the
next six days. We've got a busy week ahead of us. Day one I
thought we could put up a nice little light over there.

Son Just one?

Father Well, when I say little, I rather imagined it would be sort of
well . . . the sun. You know, not so much "little", more . . .
massively huge and gigantic. Day two . . .

Son Hang on. Is that it? For day one? Is that all?

Father Oh yes, that's plenty for day one. Now day two I thought we
could pin up a little blue curtain over there. Sort of about the
size of the entire sky. Yes. In fact it would be the sky. The
whole works. Sun and sky. Goes rather well together doesn't
it?

Son Sun, sky . . . sea and . . . sand! All the s's . . . I could sort that
out over there . . .

Father	Hang on! Wait a minute. Wait a minute. You're going too fast. Don't jump the gun. I'm coming to that joke in a minute. Ahem. Day three. Sun, sky, sea and sand. All the s's? Quite good isn't it?
Son	Yes, Dad.
Father	I thought you could work on a bit of earth.
Son	How much earth?
Father	Well, all of it. Earth, the planet. In fact – we'll have lots of planets everywhere. Put them all around the sun and then give them a few solar systems after coffee. After lunch we can think about whether to have life on Mars.
Son	And day four?
Father	Oh well, day four is going to take quite some time.
Son	Time?
Father	Yes. It's what day four's all about. We're gonna make some time. We'll put the moon up there, with a little sort of cheesy effect, and then we'll have the sun of course, and I quite like the idea of lots of stars that you can see at night.
Son	What's night?
Father	Ah, that's the opposite to day.
Son	And what's day?
Both	The opposite to night.
Son	Yes I thought you might say that.
Father	We're going to make all these fantastic little lights in the sky which you can see in the dark. I've been out and bought a few million bulbs. The ones that last for several years. We can replace them as time goes by. In the day people will see by the sun.
Son	Just one question. What's people?
Father	Ah, you're jumping ahead again. Let's go to day five first. Sea monsters and dinosaurs, and vampire bats, and rottweilers. They're all creatures, son. I can't wait for day five. I've shipped in a skip load of play dough, we can make anything

| | we like to fill the earth. All kinds of animals and fish and birds. All you have to do is think of a name and we can make it. Go on, try it – think of something. |

Son   Anything?

Father Anything. Any name you like. Doesn't matter how weird and wonderful.

(*Son thinks.*)

Son   Chihuahua.

Father Not bad, not bad.

Son   Duck-bill platypus.

Father Excellent. You see now you're on a roll.

Son   The Loch Ness monster.

Father Oh now you're being ridiculous.

Son   Sorry.

Father Okay, day six. The big one. Imagine if you will, the most incredible thing ever. Something too big for words, something so fantastic that it'll blow your mind. Imagine, if you can, something, someone like . . .

Son   Yes?

Father You. And me.

Son   What?

Father That's it. We're going to fill the planet with people. That's what people are. Made in our image. Made like us. And you know the best bit? We can be their friends. They're gonna be our friends. We'll talk with them and laugh and debate, and we'll have parties under the trees and picnics by the streams and rivers.

Son   Suppose they don't want us to be their friends.

Father Oh they will! They're bound to, when they see what we've made and given to them. Honest – it'll be paradise.

Son   What's paradise?

Father Oh! I'm not sure.

(*He flicks through the book.*)

Father Here we are it's . . . Well, (*He looks round*) this actually. Heaven. Oh now look. This is my favourite day. Day seven.

Son You mean there's still more to come?

Father No.

Son No?

Father No. On day seven we invent . . . breakfast in bed. It's the day off. It's the big one. It's the day we work hard . . . at resting. And even better, the people get one too. We'll build a whole stack of days off for them so they can have one every week. If we're having a holiday then they get one too. It'll be a day when people and God can take it easy together. What do you think?

(*They both freeze.*)

The Bible

The Good Ol' Book

Bible references

Exodus 37-42, Joshua 6, Judges 6 and 7, Judges 16, 1 Samuel 17

Themes

The Bible; the Old Testament heroes and villains

Cast

One or two narrators who deliver the words in a rapping style
Two people, namely 1 and 2, who illustrate the narrative

The narrative may be delivered to a rhythm if so desired.

Narrator/s Back down the road, way back in time,

(1 and 2 walk on, see the audience and wave.)

      When life had a rhythm and a reason and a rhyme.

(1 walks to the front of the stage and mimes opening a large book.)

      They wrote a good book – and called it the Bible,

(They mime reading the book.)

      It had Joseph, Jonah, and Goliath inside it.

(2 taps 1 on the shoulder, beckons to him and they get ready to illustrate the stories.)

      Joseph had a coat, a coat of many colours

(1 mimes putting a coat on 2, 2 smooths out any wrinkles.)

      A present from his old man – did not impress his brothers.

(1 looks angry and jealous.)

      They sold him as a slave, left him on his own

(1 grabs 2 by the shoulder, 2 looks worried.)

But ten years later he was sittin' on a throne.

(*1 lets go of 2 and drops onto his knees, grovelling before Joseph.*)

Movin' on a bit, we come to a town,

(*Step forward and look around.*)

Where Josh and his mates had to walk around and round.

(*Walk around each other.*)

They blew on their trumpets and the wall fell down

(*Mime playing trumpets.*)

God lent a hand and brought it crashing down.

(*Look up, then look horrified and duck down, hands covering heads.*)

Then there was Gideon hiding underground

(*1 mimes opening a trapdoor and climbing inside.*)

He was scared stiff he was gonna be found.

(*1 crouches down and bites nails, 2 searches around for 1.*)

But an angel caught him and gave him a job

(*2 opens the trapdoor and points at 1, 1 looks shocked.*)

And he found he could do amazing things with God.

(*1 climbs out and shakes hands with 2.*)

So Gideon survived to tell the tale,

(*1 wipes brow and looks relieved, 2 pats him on the back.*)

Just like Jonah sittin' in the whale,

(*2 mimes sitting and looking around worried.*)

The whale swallowed Jonah when he tried to run away

(*1 mimes taking a huge bite and chews enthusiastically, 2 jumps and twitches around.*)

Then threw up on the beach and spoilt his day.

(*1 mimes being sick and pushes 2 forward and onto the floor.*)

Then came a strong man – Samson was his name.

(2 flexes muscles and strikes a pose.)

He fell in love with a hair-cutting dame.

(1 points offstage at imaginary woman, 2 looks, wilts and goes all shy.)

She was called Delilah – when he fell asleep

(2 falls asleep and snores.)

She gave him a trim and his knees turned weak.

(1 wakes 2 hurriedly, 2 wakes up, looks at his hair and collapses.)

Here's another strong man – Goliath he was called.

(1 looks mean, paces up and down and pulls faces at the audience.)

He thought he was the toughest bruiser of them all.

(1 mimes punching 2 and 2 falls over.)

Then a little boy called Dave came along –

(2 crawls in on his knees.)

Hit him on the head and he wasn't so strong.

(2 fires a catapult at 1, 1 looks stunned and staggers.)

There are many more in the Good Ol' Book

(2 walks to stage front and mimes opening a large book.)

Let your fingers do the walking and take a look.

(1 comes over and runs his fingers along the page as they read it together.)

With Joshua, Joseph and Gide-on.

(1 and 2 look amazed.)

The adventures just roll on and on . . .

(Both freeze.)

Two juggling parables

The unforgiving juggler

Bible references

Matthew 18. 21-35: the parable of the unforgiving servant

Themes

Treating people fairly and honestly; forgiving as we have been forgiven

Cast

Shop owner
Juggler
Friend

Begin with the juggler walking on and juggling with a large variety of things: clubs, balls, sticks, plates, whatever. He may use a unicycle too, any other circus skills and props. Enter the shop owner who watches for a moment then speaks.

Shop owner　　That's brilliant. You're amazing.

Juggler　　Thanks.

Shop owner　　Yes. Now that's £5,000 you owe me.

(Juggler is so shocked he drops whatever he is juggling at the time.)

Juggler　　What!!!?

Shop owner　　Well, so far you've had 37 clubs, 20 unicycles, 15 fire sticks, 4 chainsaws, 300 plates, 794 juggling balls and 2 tightropes – all from my shop, and you haven't paid me anything. That's £5,000 please.

(Juggler looks in his pockets then shrugs.)

Juggler　　But – I don't have any money.

Shop owner　　Oh!

(*He thinks for a minute.*)

Shop owner   I'll tell you what, you can keep it all – for nothing. I like you and you're a great juggler so keep everything. Have it all as a gift, go and make lots of people happy.

Juggler   Thanks!

(*Juggler picks up his stuff and walks over to one side of the stage. Shop owner exits and the friend enters.*)

Friend   Hi! I haven't see you for ages. How are you?

Juggler   Great! I've just been given all this stuff. Shall I show what I can do?

Friend   Yes, please.

(*So the juggler does some of his act. At the end the friend applauds loudly.*)

Friend   Brilliant, thanks. See ya! (*He goes to leave.*)

Juggler   Wait a minute. Where are you going?

Friend   I've got to go . . .

Juggler   Not until you've paid me.

Friend   Paid you?

Juggler   Yes. You had . . . (*Checks his watch.*) Two minutes and twenty seconds of entertainment . . . That's £5 you owe me.

Friend   £5! For that?!

Juggler   Yes. Now pay up.

Friend   I can't. I'm broke. I haven't any money.

Juggler   Right. Okay. In that case, I'll have . . . (*He looks him up and down.*) Your watch . . . your coat . . . and your trainers, please.

(*The friend is shocked but sadly takes these off and hands them over. Then he wanders away sadly.*)

Juggler   Thanks very much.

(*He turns to walk off in the other direction and bumps into the shop owner coming back on stage.*)

Shop owner	Hello. How's it going?
Juggler	Great! I got a new coat, and a watch.
Shop owner	Where did you get those?
Juggler	Oh my friend owed me £5 for a juggling show, but he didn't have any money so he gave me these.
Shop owner	What! That's terrible!
Juggler	Yea, not much of a deal was it?
Shop owner	I don't mean that! I let you off a debt of £5,000 – and you took all this from someone who only owed you £5?
Juggler	Oh! Well . . .
Shop owner	No excuses! In that case, working on the same calculations – you owe me . . . 1,000 watches, 1,000 coats and 1,000 . . . er no . . . 500 trainers.
Juggler	But I don't have all those. You know that!
Shop owner	Oh don't you, indeed? Well in that case, I'll have all that juggling equipment back – everything – until you pay me in full.

(*He leads the juggler off by the scruff of the neck.*)

The persistent juggler

Bible references
Luke 18.1-8: the parable of the persistent widow

Themes
Persistence; friendship; patience; endurance

Cast
Juggler
Learner

Juggler walks on juggling. Learner walks up to him and watches for a while, then speaks:

Learner   Hey! That's good. That's really good.

Juggler   Shh . . . you'll break my concentration.

(*Learner watches for a little while longer.*)

Learner   Can you teach me to do that?

Juggler   No.

Learner   Oh, why not?

Juggler   Because I'm busy. Go away.

(*Learner walks off sadly. Juggler continues, then Learner walks back on.*)

Learner   Can you teach me now?

Juggler   No.

Learner   Please.

Juggler   No.

(*Learner watches then shakes Juggler, making him drop the balls.*)

Juggler   What is it!!

Learner   Will you teach me now?

Juggler   No. Go away.

(*Pause. Then Learner catches one of Juggler's balls.*)

Learner   Look, I can do it with one . . .

(*Juggler snatches it back.*)

Juggler   I'll do you in a minute . . . Now go home.

(*Learner watches then taps Juggler on the shoulder and points and shouts:*)

Learner   Look over there!

(*Juggler looks, dropping the balls in the process. Learner quickly scoops them up and tries to juggle, he drops them all.*)

Juggler   See! You can't do it.

Learner   Can.

Juggler   Can't.

Learner   I can . . . if you teach me.

Juggler   No.

Learner   Oh . . . Pleeeeeeeeeeeeeease.

(*Juggler starts juggling again. Learner walks close to him and shouts in his ear:*)

Learner   Pleeeeeeeeeeeeeeeeeeeeeeeeeeeeeeeeeeeeeeeeeeeeeeeeease!!!!!!

(*Juggler drops all the balls and leaps in the air.*)

Juggler   Oh for goodness sake all right. You're driving me up the wall. Yes! Whatever you want – yes! Here, try this . . .

Learner   Thanks! See I can do it with one ball . . .

(*They walk off together.*)

Giving and taking

Love is like this . . .

Bible references
1 Corinthians 13

Themes
Love, friendship and support

Cast
Narrator
Four actors: 1, 2, 3 and 4

Narrator
Love is like this.

(*1 and 2 meet and shake hands.*)

But it's not like this.

(*3 and 4 strangle each other.*)

Love is like this.

(*1 and 2 share some food.*)

But it's not like this.

(*3 picks 4's pocket.*)

Love is like this.

(*1 trips and is caught by 2.*)

But it's not like this.

(*3 trips and 4 laughs.*)

Love is like this.

(*1 helps 2 who pretends to be a blind person.*)

But it's never like this.

(*3 puts a foot out to trip 4 up.*)

Love is like this.

(*1, 2 and 3 talk together, 4 is alone looking fed up. 1 pulls 4 into the group.*)

But it's not like this.

(*1, 2 and 3 pull faces at 4.*)

Love is not very easy sometimes.

(*1 and 3 try hard to reach out to 2 and 4.*)

But this is very easy.

(*1 and 3 turn their backs and 2 and 4 fall over.*)

Love makes people feel better.

(*They pat each other on the back.*)

Not worse.

(*1 pushes 2 down, 4 pushes 3 down.*)

Love can help in every situation.

(*1 and 4 pull the others up.*)

It is the most important thing in the world.

(*They hug each other and all freeze.*)

Zac

Bible references
Luke 19.1-10

Themes
Friendship with Jesus; a changed life

Cast
Zac
Woman 1
Man
Woman 2

Zac	S'cuse me madam. Can I have a quick word?
Woman 1	What? How dare you! Don't be absurd!
	I'm in a hurry – now go away! (*She marches off.*)
Zac	(*To audience*) Look at that. Well what can you say?
	Ah s'cuse me, sir. I'm out here today
	Giving lots of free gifts away.
Man	Oh no, not another special offer, get lost.
Zac	Give me just a minute, there'll be no cost.
Man	I don't want what you're selling. You can keep it, mate.
Zac	But it's absolutely free. Listen, wait!
Man	Absolutely?
Zac	Absolutely. I promise you that.
Man	It's not dog food is it? Or something for the cat?
Zac	No!

Man   'Cause I'm allergic to dogs. And I'm scared of cats.

And little furry animals and vampire bats.

And I'm allergic to mice. Hamsters and cars.

And washing powder. And crisps. And cigars.

Zac   It's nothing to do with any of them.

Man   Oh! All right – what is it then?

(*Zac pulls out a five pound note.*)

Man   I thought you said it wasn't about cash.

Oh dear is that the time – I really must dash.

Zac   You see how difficult it is? I'll have one more shot.

Oi! S'cuse me, Madam.

Woman 2   Yes? What?

Zac   May I give something to you?

Woman 2   Why?

Zac   A friend of mine told me to.

Woman 2   What friend?

Zac   Jesus. I met him up a tree.

Woman 2   What was he doing up there – up a tree?

Zac   No he wasn't up a tree, that was me.

I was the one who was up the tree.

Woman 2   Why?

Zac   Because I couldn't see.

Woman 2   Well, no wonder – if you were stuck up a tree.

What a silly place to be.

Zac   But I couldn't see. I was far too small,

I just couldn't see him at all.

There was a crowd of people standing in the way,

And they'd been waiting for him all day.

	Then I went up the tree and I could see.
Woman 2	Who is he then?
Zac	He's my best friend. He's an amazing bloke.
	Very kind, very understanding, and he tells a darn good joke.
	And he tells lots of great stories too.
Woman 2	Oh? And what did he say to you?
Zac	He said I should give my money away.
	So I've been stuck out here all day.
	You see I'm pretty rich, but I stole it all.
	When it comes to being naughty I'm really on the ball.
	But now I've changed I've turned over a new leaf,
	But it's not easy giving away money when everyone thinks you're a thief.
	So will you take this fiver and help me out?

(*She takes the money.*)

Woman 2	Well, if you insist and could you tell me about . . .
Zac	About what?
Woman 2	About him. This brand new friend.
Zac	I can't, 'cause this sketch is about to end.
	But I'll tell you what I think I'll do.
	I'll take you to see him and you can meet him too.
Woman 2	Excellent!
Zac	Oh! What rhymes with excellent? Oh dear, we've run out of rhymes, drat . . .
Woman 2	Sorry.
Zac	Don't worry, they might not have noticed. Quick let's slip off – for a cup of coff – ee. Bye!

(*They exit.*)

Telling the truth – light and darkness

Frisk and Dexter
and the lie detector

Bible references
1 Kings 3.16-28

Themes
Truth and lies; the wisdom of King Solomon

Cast
Narrator
Frisk
Dexter

Narrator Frisk and Dexter ran a time travel investigation agency. They were detectives who could investigate any crime from any time. When the purple phone on Dexter's desk rang like an old school bell, they knew that a case from history was calling them.

Dexter wore a long black coat and had a dog called Bilko.

(*Dexter walks on wearing a long black coat. He mimes pulling a dog on a lead.*)

Frisk wore small, dark glasses and always carried a notebook.

(*Frisk walks on putting on his dark glasses.*)

One day the purple phone rang . . .

(*Dexter mimes picking up a phone.*)

And Frisk and Dexter found themselves standing at the foot of a huge temple.

(*They look around astonished.*)

Frisk had brought his lie detector along just in case, as he had a feeling he might need it.

(*He mimes holding it and says 'Beep beep!' as he switches it on.*)

As they stood looking, two woman pushed past them and marched into the temple carrying a baby between them.

(*They jump aside as two imaginary women push past them.*)

Frisk   Quick follow them!

Narrator   Said Frisk. So they did. Inside they went into a very large room full of shining gold and sparkling jewels.

(*They push through two big doors and stand staring.*)

Dexter   Wow!

(*Frisk mimes picking up a handful of jewels.*)

Narrator   Sitting in the room, on a big throne was a king called Solomon.

(*They bow down.*)

'King Solomon,' said one of the women. 'This woman has stolen my baby.'

(*Frisk and Dexter stand up and look stage left as she speaks.*)

'No I haven't', said the other woman, 'she stole my baby'.

(*They look stage right and watch the other one. Then they look at each other and shrug.*)

Both women pretended to be the mother.

Dexter   Who's telling the truth?

Narrator   Asked Dexter.

Frisk switched on his lie detector.

(*Frisk does this and says 'Beep beep!'*)

But before he could say anything King Solomon spoke up.

'I know what to do,' he said, 'Get a big sword and cut the baby in two pieces then you can have half each'.

(*Frisk and Dexter look horrified.*)

One of the women nodded and agreed,

(*They look stage left and look amazed, Frisk starts to intervene but Dexter pulls him back.*)

But the other one said, 'No! Don't do that! Give the baby to the other woman.'

(*They look stage right.*)

King Solomon smiled. 'No', he said. 'You can have the baby, because you must be the real mother if you didn't want to hurt the child.'

Frisk looked at the lie detector.

Frisk   He's right. She's the one telling the truth.

(*He points to stage right.*)

Narrator   They checked their watches.

(*They do this.*)

It was time to get back to the future.

(*They run on the spot.*)

As they went Frisk wrote the case down in his notebook. He called it the case of the two mothers and the very wise king.

(*Frisk freezes scribbling in his diary. Dexter looks at the audience and winks knowingly.*)

Frisk and Dexter
and the boy in the well

Bible references
Genesis 37.1-28

Themes
The story of Joseph; God's ways are not our ways

Cast
Narrator

Frisk

Dexter

Narrator   Frisk and Dexter ran a time travel investigation agency. They were detectives who could investigate any crime from any time. When the purple phone on Dexter's desk rang like an old school bell, they knew that a case from history was calling them.

Dexter wore a long black coat and had a dog called Bilko.

(*Dexter walks on wearing a long black coat. He mimes pulling a dog on a lead.*)

Frisk wore small, dark glasses and always carried a notebook.

(*Frisk walks on putting on his dark glasses.*)

One day the purple phone rang . . .

(*Dexter mimes picking up a phone.*)

And Frisk and Dexter found themselves sweating in the middle of a hot desert.

(*They look around and wipe their brows with their handkerchiefs then wring them out.*)

Frisk was grateful for his dark glasses as the sun beat down like a massive spotlight,

(*Frisk takes off his glasses, blows dust off them, puts them back on and smooths back his hair.*)

But Dexter threw off his long black coat and left it lying in the dust.

(*Dexter peels off his coat and tosses it over his shoulder, it hits Frisk.*)

They began to walk.

Frisk   Where now, boss?

Narrator   Asked Frisk, flicking open his notebook and beginning to scribble in it.

(*Frisk scribbles in his book. Dexter stops suddenly.*)

Dexter   Listen!

(*Frisk walks into him and drops the notebook in surprise.*)

Narrator   Dexter stopped so suddenly that Frisk walked into him, and Bilko walked into Frisk.

(*Frisk makes a yelping sound and he and Dexter look back at Bilko and say: 'Ssshhhh!'*)

As they listened they heard the sound of a cry.

(*They lean together and place a hand to their ears.*)

Frisk pointed to an old muddy well and they ran towards it like kids running for an ice cream van.

(*Frisk points stage left and they run on the spot facing that direction.*)

They stopped and looked in, a young teenager lay at the bottom, his body crunched up and splashes of blood smeared on his face and clothes. The situation looked dangerous.

(*They stop running and look into an imaginary hole. Dexter looks around cautiously.*)

Frisk   (*In a loud whisper.*) Someone's thrown him in.

Narrator   Whispered Frisk, still scribbling in his notebook.

(*Frisk searches for his notebook but he has lost it and he shrugs at the audience and shakes his head.*)

Dexter wondered why they were whispering, and he whispered this back to Frisk.

(*Dexter whispers in Frisk's ear, this tickles Frisk and he shivers and rubs his ear.*)

They looked around, the place was deserted.

(*They look around, their hands above their eyes.*)

Frisk   Sorry, thought the guys who threw him in might still be around.

Narrator   Dexter tried to reach inside the well to pull the boy out, but it was way too deep.

(*Dexter tries to reach down while Frisk hangs onto his leg.*)

Frisk   Here boss, try this old bit of rag.

Narrator   Frisk had picked up Dexter's black coat.

(*Dexter looks at the coat then at Frisk and he slaps Frisk on the arm and folds the coat up nicely. Then he hands it back to Frisk, Frisk looks at it then shrugs and throws it over his shoulder again.*)

Dexter decided there was only one thing for it.

Dexter   I'm going down there myself.

Narrator   He said, rolling his sleeves up. But Frisk grabbed him.

(*Dextor rolls his sleeves up, but Frisk grabs him.*)

Frisk pointed off into the distance, a long wiry line of camels appeared on the skyline. The riders looked mean, and dangerous.

(*Frisk points off stage left.*)

Dexter   No time to waste.

Narrator   Said Dexter.

Dexter   If we don't get him, those guys will.

Narrator   But Frisk stopped him again. He pointed down inside the well, towards the boy's coat. It lay next to him and it was all the colours of the rainbow.

(*Frisk points down into the well again.*)

Frisk   I don't think we should rescue him, Boss. I have a hunch this boy's gonna go to Egypt and get a top job in government.

Narrator   Dexter wasn't so sure. He looked at the coat with all its colours, then at the line of camels.

(Dexter scratches his head and looks at the well, then off stage at the approaching men.)

They looked mean, and very dangerous. Suddenly ten men appeared from nowhere.

(Frisk and Dexter back up against each other and rotate on the spot looking at the ten men all around them.)

They were the boy's brothers.

Dexter   Of course! The boy in the well is called Joseph, and these are his brothers. They've come to get him out!

Narrator   Frisk and Dexter made a run for it.

Frisk   Let's get back to the future, quick!

(They grab Dexter's coat and Frisk's notebook and run on the spot.)

Narrator   As they ran back to the 1990s, still sweating from the desert heat, Frisk noted in his book that sometimes it was better to leave things for God to work out. He had special plans for Joseph, and if they'd pulled him from the well things might have gone very wrong indeed . . .

(Frisk and Dexter freeze.)

Light and dark – a responsive sermon

Bible references
John 8. 12

Themes
Light and darkness

Cast
One reader/speaker

You may like to try this responsive sermon, or create your own all-involving sermon. Either way, teach the following key words and responses to the congregation before beginning.

Key words:
light – *say: 'Click!'*
dark – *screw up eyes*
fireworks – *say: 'Whizz bang!'*
spotlight – *look dazzled*
candle – *hold one up*
robot/s – *move like a robot*
see – *cover eyes with hand then uncover them and say 'Ding!'*
sunglasses – *look cool and say: 'Hey!'*

Now, Jesus said that he is the **light**.

That means he can show us the way, and make things safe, like using a torch in the **dark**.

Now he also wants to shine his **light** through us. Through you and me. That's what being a Christian is all about. You see, for a lot of people life is a bit like being in the **dark**, and they feel a bit scared, and they really need a **light**.

So, as Jesus helps us to **see** which way to go, so we can help others to **see** which way to go. And Jesus can use us whether we're very old or very young. But being a Christian doesn't mean we all have to be the same, Jesus doesn't want us to be like **robots**.

He wants to shine his **light** through each of us in different ways. Think about this for a moment; at Christmas we use **candles**; on Guy Fawkes night we use **fireworks**; and at the theatre they have very big **spotlights**.

They're all very different, but they all bring **light** into the **dark**.

In the same way – we're all different:

some of us might be like a little gentle **candle**.

Some of us might be like a noisy **firework** –

or we might be like a powerful **spotlight**.

But whoever we are Jesus wants to give us his **light**

so that we can shine out for him. Not by trying to be something we're not, like **robots** – but by being ourselves, and getting to know Jesus better and better.

One last thing. Sometimes it's **dark** –

not because we don't have a **candle**, or a **spotlight**

– but because we're wearing **sunglasses**.

Now **sunglasses** are cool

but they do block out the **light**

and make it difficult to **see**.

So, in a similar way, we have to keep asking God to help us with anything we have in our lives which might block out his amazing **light**.

God gives us things we can do

Gifts

Bible references
Matthew 25.14-30

Themes
The talents and abilities we all possess, sharing these
and supporting one another; the parable of the talents.

Cast
Narrator
A group of 4 who respond to the narrative
with the actions described below in italics.

Narrator   Some people are good at sport,
(All mime playing a different sport.)

Some people are good at cooking,
(Make sizzling sound and pretend to fry an egg.)

Some people are good at thinking,
(All say 'Ugh . . .' as if thinking.)

Some people are good at gardening.
(All say: 'Ooh arr!')

Some like writing,
(Mime writing.)

Some like reading,
(All say: 'Once upon a time . . .' as if telling a story.)

Some like running,

(Crouch into a starting position.)

A lot of us like watching television.

(Stare wide-eyed at an imaginary television set.)

Jesus told a story about three people who were good at different things.

(All listen, placing a hand to ear.)

They were each given some money.

(All hold out one hand and take money.)

Two of them thought carefully,

(All say 'Ugh . . .' as if thinking.)

Wrote down their ideas,

(Mime writing.)

And then worked like mad to make it all happen.

The first one bought a dinosaur theme park.

(All pretend to be dinosaurs and roar ferociously. The narrator looks very scared indeed.)

It was very popular and many people came to see it.

(All bunch together like a crowd, look around in awe and say 'Ooh! Aah!' Then they take photos and all say 'Click! Click!' as they press the buttons on their cameras.)

The second one bought a lot of equipment and invented an inflatable . . . *(Pause)*

(All make blowing noises and pretend to inflate something.)

Cow!

(All say 'Mmmmmooooooooooooo!')

It always gave perfect milk and never got any horrible diseases. And when you shook it up . . .

(All bounce up and down on the spot saying a trembly sounding 'M . . .m . . .m . . .oooo!')

It produced a delicious milk shake!

(*All lick lips and say: 'Mmmmmm! Yummy'.*)

He sold millions of these inflatable cows and made a lot of profit. He worked very hard.

(*All wipe brow, look tired and collapse on one another in a heap.*)

But the other one didn't. He had a nice rest,

(*All stay on the floor in a heap, sleeping and snoring loudly.*)

Then he woke up

(*Wake up, stretch and yawn.*)

And had a great idea.

(*All stand up, raise a finger and say: 'Ding!'*)

He decided to do . . . nothing!

(*All fall asleep again, drop to the floor and snore.*)

So, two of them used their gifts really well.

(*All stand up. One of the group becomes a dinosaur again and the others applaud. Then another of the group says 'Mooo!' and the others turn to them and applaud.*)

But the third one didn't. And in the end – he lost everything.

(*All turn out pockets and look sad.*)

We can all do different things.

(*Some mime writing, some doing sport, some gardening, etc.*)

And everybody is good at something.

(*All applaud each other, and pat each other on the back. Then all freeze.*)

So it's important to do the best we can. And to help others do the same.

(*All freeze doing different things again. Some writing, some doing sport, some gardening, some being dinosaurs, etc.*)

Gideon and the angel

Bible references
Judges 6 and 7

Themes
Angels; the power of God; trusting in God; laying out a fleece

Cast
Narrator
Angel, cool, James Bond type
Gideon, scared stiff

Narrator walks on and stands stage left.

Narrator   Once there was an angel

(*Enter the angel, wearing a black bow tie and sunglasses, and carrying a water pistol. The narrator watches. James Bond theme music plays in the background. The angel creeps around.*)

And there was a water pistol.

(*Angel creeps stealthily around the narrator and audience, perhaps threatening to squirt one or two, perhaps squirting them all!*)

Now an angel is like a special agent – a sort of spy who works for God.

But angels don't normally carry water pistols.

(*The angel looks disappointed.*)

However, the angel in our story was called Bond, Gabriel Bond and his code name was double-o-heaven, and he was on a special mission.

(*Angel holds the pistol across his chest in a James Bond pose – the pistol squirts by mistake and he jumps. The music fades out.*)

102

Now. Meet Gideon – he was hiding inside a paper bag, because he was a nervous chap.

(*Enter Gideon with a large paper bag on his head and wearing a jacket.*)

But double-o-heaven found him

(*Angel puts his hand on Gideon's shoulder, Gideon jumps.*)

and told him that God had a very special mission for him to do.

(*Angel whispers in Gideon's ear. Gideon thinks then shakes head. Angel whispers. Gideon shakes his head. The angel thinks and scratches his head.*)

Gideon was too scared to do the job because he felt he wasn't very good at doing anything.

Gabriel told him that God would help him, he didn't have to do it on his own.

Gideon thought about this then he had a bright idea.

Gideon (*Incomprehensibly from inside the bag.*) Mmmrrffmmffm, mrmr-mmsggfdjnfmm, vjjfigsndk, dmuhgmkvbnmdhshudnl;fbjkj.

(*Angel thinks for a minute.*)

Angel He said: 'I've got a bright idea – if God can do a miracle for me I'll know I can trust him to help me'.

Gideon Mmrmmfoshb jfhjdn.

Angel He said, 'that's right.'

Narrator So Gideon whispered his plan in the angel's ear.

(*Gideon whispers in angel's ear.*)

Angel Right. (*Gideon puts his jacket on the ground.*) This is the miracle.

(*Gideon whispers to the angel again.*)

Narrator And Gideon asked the angel if – while he was asleep – God could make the coat wet with rain, but leave all the rest of the ground bone dry.

So he went to sleep.

(*Gideon snores. Angel places finger and thumb over his nose to stop him. Then the angel pulls out the pistol and squirts the jacket.*)

And in the morning,

(*Angel makes alarm clock sound. Gideon leaps out of his skin and slaps the angel round the head to stop him. Gideon rushes to his jacket feels it and his mouth drops open. He examines the floor, smells it, runs his finger over it, licks it, he looks amazed.*)

Gideon was amazed. (*Gideon nods.*) The angel of course knew how it was done. But that's what a miracle is – something we can't do and God can. Then Gideon asked for another miracle.

(*Gideon whispers to angel.*)

Only this time he wanted the ground wet with rain and the jacket dry.

(*Gideon sleeps again. The angel squirts the floor, sighs, then squirts Gideon who is snoring again. Gideon wakes with a shudder and a jump.*)

And the next morning. Bingo!

(*Gideon wakes and sees the miracle.*)

Now, it's a long story . . .

(*Angel and Gideon fall asleep and snore.*)

But basically Gideon decided to do the job that God asked him to do.

(*Gideon wakes up, rips off the bag, leaps in the air with karate chops and kicks.*)

But – he didn't suddenly turn into a Power Ranger.

(*Gideon looks sheepish. Angel puts arm round Gideon. Freeze side by side.*)

Instead in his own small way, he did what God wanted – and God helped him.

(*All exit happily.*)

Families

Joe and his brothers

Bible references
Genesis 37, 42 and 45

Themes
Dreams; jealousy; betrayal; families; forgiveness

Cast
Joe
Brother 1
Brother 2
Brother 3

This is a piece of physical theatre, i.e. lively, loud and energetic. It moves along at a good pace and quickly switches from one picture or scene to another.

Begin with 4 people in a line, standing with their backs to the audience as below:

1   2   3   4   *(Joe)*

Brother 2 blows a whistle and all the others jump round and say:

> Here's a story, you might just know
> It's about some brothers and a guy called Joe.

(Joe steps forward and says:)

Joe   I am Joseph I'm Jacob's child.

I had a dream last night and it was really wild.

(Joe freezes. The brothers step forward and say:)

Brothers 1, 2 and 3 Oh no. Not a dream. Oh no. Not another.

We've had it up to here with our dear little brother.

(The brothers repeat their lines together three times as Brother 1 gets them all together, Brothers 2 and 3 sitting on chairs as in a classroom. Brother 1 clears his throat and they all look attentive.)

Brother 1   Right – we need – to teach him – a lesson!

Brothers 2 and 3   Right – we need – to teach him – a lesson!

(All say this two more times.)

Brothers 1, 2 and 3 *(Sweetly)* Oh Joseph!

Joe   *(Equally sweetly)* Oh brothers!

(All then clap their hands twice and then say 'Here', and point to the stage in front of them. Joe walks over saying:)

Joe   I am Joseph I am Jacob's child.

                       I had a dream last night and it was really wild.

Brother 1   Right lads – grab the prisoner.

(Joe turns to the audience and happily repeats:)

Joe   Right lads – grab the prisoner. Wait a minute? What prisoner?

Brothers   You!

(And they point at him, push their chairs back violently and begin to circle him.)

Joe   I dreamt last night about a field – it was sunny

                       You all bowed down to me – now isn't that funny?

Brothers   No it isn't . . . Let's do him. Let's sort him out

                       Let's turn him into raspberry jam and spread him all about.

(They all begin to look around for a hole, including Joe, all chanting together as they search:)

Brothers   Find a hole – find a pit – and put him in it.

                       Find a hole – find a pit – and put him in it.

                       Find a hole – find a pit – and put him in it.

                       Find a hole – find a pit – and put . . .

Joe	(*Shouts out and points to the floor at his own feet.*) Got one!
Brother 1	Little brother – you're a genius!
Brother 2	There's only one word for you.
Joe	What's that?
Brothers	(*With a big smile.*) Goodbye!

(*And they push him down to a crouching position and sit on him. Brother 1 stands up and begins to pace and says:*)

Brother 1	Oh dear – oh dear – we can't leave him here.
Brother 2	(*Stands up and joins in.*) Oh dear – oh dear – we can't leave him here.
Brother 3	(*Also stands up and joins in.*) Oh dear – oh dear – we can't leave him here.
Brother 1	Oh dear – oh dear – oh wait, I've got it.
	Let's sell him as a slave and live off the profit.
Brothers	Yea! Sell him as a slave and live off the profit.
	Sell him as a slave and live off the profit.
	If we leave him here he might just cop it.
	So we'll we sell him as a slave and live off the profit!
Brother	Oh Joseph! (*Sweetly.*)
Joe	(*Looking up for the first time.*) Yes? (*Hopefully.*)
Brothers	Come here!

(*The brothers pull Joe up and freeze holding him.*)

(*Brother 3 steps away from the others and says:*)

Brother 3	So we sold him as a slave and pretended he was dead
	Joe went to Egypt and we went to bed.

(*Joe exits. Brothers 1 and 2 lean on each other, back to back and snore.*)

Brother 3	Here is the news.
	There'll be sun all day – it'll beat on the street.

It'll be very hot and you won't have much to eat.

The corn will wither and the sun will fry it

There'll be no food around and you'll all be on a diet.

(*Then Brothers 1 and 2 wake up and say:*)

Brothers 1 and 2	Famine!
Brother 3	However.

In Egypt they've got an awful lot stored up

So why not take a holiday and fill your tummies up?

Brother 1	Quick! Start packing.
Brothers 2 and 3	Right! Start packing.
Brother 1	On second thoughts . . . Quick! Stop packing.
Brothers	Right! Stop packing.
Brother 1	We need room in the cases to bring the food back.
Brothers	(*Singing*)

'We're all going on a Summer holiday . . .'

(*They stand as if on a bus holding cases and holding onto hand rails.*)

Brother 1	We're here!

(*They leap off and bow down.*)

Brothers	We're not nice people and we're often rude and crude

But please have mercy and give us lots of food.

(*They repeat this. Joe walks on again.*)

Joe	I dreamt last night about a field – it was sunny

You all bowed down to me – now isn't that funny?

(*The brothers look up.*)

Brothers	Joe! It's you!
Joe	Brothers! It's me!

I am Joseph I am Jacob's child

I'm the boss round here now and it is really wild.

I've had a lot of dreams and they have all come true

But this is the best one, meeting up with you!

Brothers   Hey Joe we're really sorry

Hey Joe we're really bad

Hey Joe we really hurt you

Hey Joe we're really sad.

Now would you mind giving us some food, please, please, please, please . . . PLEASE!

(*They look up to Joe all begging and pleading.*)

Joe   (*Sitting down.*)

Well now brothers you all deserve to starve.

You sold me as a slave and you thought it was a laugh.

Hmmm.

(*Joe nods and the brothers look hopeful.*)

Hmmm.

(*Joe shakes his head and the brothers look unhopeful.*)

Hmmm.

(*Joe nods again and the brothers look hopeful again.*)

No.

Brothers   No!

Joe   No.

(*The brothers shake their heads and start to leave.*)

Joe   No. I can't let you starve, in spite of what you did.

111

Though you sold me as a slave when I was just a kid.

I forgive you for selling me and leaving me to die.

I won't mention it again 'cause I'm that kind of guy!

Bring everybody here, bring the mum and dad

And we'll have the biggest party anybody ever had.

Brother 3   So Joe and his brothers lived together once again.

Joe forgave them all and they were happy men.

Ding! Click!

(*They all freeze bunching together with big smiles as if posing for a family photograph.*)

Families

Bible references
Ephesians 6.1-4, Proverbs 14.26

Themes
Family life

Cast
Narrators 1 and 2
A group of 6 to 10 people who make
mimed pictures to accompany the narrative.

Narrator 1 is enthusiastic, Narrator 2 is quite negative. The group act after each line, freezing between each new picture.

1   Families are really important.

(The group smile at the audience and nod happily.)

2   Are they?

(All shrug and look perplexed.)

1   Oh yes. Let's just think about it for a minute.

(All think.)

2   Errrr . . . *(As if thinking aloud.)*

1   Now, some of us have big families.

(All make yourselves as tall as possible.)

2   Some have little ones.

(All crouch down.)

1   Yes. And some have noisy families.

(*All make a noise.*)

2   Some of us have quiet ones.

(*All put fingers to lips and stand on tip toe.*)

1   Yes. But whatever kind of family we have . . .

(*All smile again and nod happily.*)

2   Big, small, loud or quiet

(*They quickly recap and all get confused.*)

1   Families are there to stick by us.

(*All squash together in a tight mass.*)

2   Yea, but we don't always want to be that close.

(*Sniff each other and step away from each other.*)

1   They can support us.

(*Lean on each other in twos, back to back.*)

2   Yes, but sometimes they can let us down.

(*In these twos one steps away so the other one falls.*)

1   Of course they can. But no one's perfect.

(*Look at each other and pull a face.*)

2   Yea, but it can be boring to have to be with your family.

(*All yawn loudly.*)

1   Ah! But sometimes it can be an adventure.

(*Look excited and run about wide-eyed.*)

2   Sometimes it's just a big argument.

(*All fight.*)

1   It may not always be easy and sometimes it's very difficult.

(*All look fed up.*)

2   Yea. Sometimes you have to grit your teeth!

(*All grit teeth dramatically.*)

1   But often when we're mixed up or confused our family can point us in the right direction.

(*All point in different directions.*)

2   That's true.

(*All nod happily.*)

1   And we're all part of a much bigger family.

(*Look around and point at the audience.*)

2   Are we?

1   Yes. God's family.

(*All link hands and freeze smiling.*)

Bereavement

Losing our friends

Themes
Bereavement, losing our friends, heaven

Cast
Narrator

Two actors

Narrator   We often lose things.

(*Pat pockets and search around for something.*)

We lose our way.

(*Look lost.*)

We lose our memory.

(*Scratch heads.*)

We lose our sweets.

(*Hold stomach as if hungry.*)

And we lose our energy.

(*Collapse and fall over.*)

Sometimes we lose our friends too.

(*Push each other away as if annoyed with each other.*)

Sometimes we lose them because they go away.

(*Wave goodbye.*)

Sometimes they move to another street.

(*Step further apart and wave.*)

Or another town.

(*Step further apart again and wave.*)

Or even another country.

(*Step as far away as possible and wave, perhaps look through binoculars.*)

And sometimes they go on to another life.

(*One faces the audience and looks around for the other, the other faces away.*)

When they go to another street we can go there for tea.

(*Mime eating and drinking together.*)

When they go to another town we can call them on the phone.

(*Step further apart and mime a phone conversation.*)

When they to another country we can write them a letter on special blue paper.

(*Step further apart and mime writing furiously then fold the letter and throw it like a paper aeroplane to each other and both read them.*)

When they go to another life we can talk to God about them

(*Both pray quietly.*)

And tell him when we miss them.

(*One look sad the other look fed up.*)

Then one day, when we go there too, we will see them again.

(*Hug each other happily.*)

Lazarus

Bible references
John 11.1-44

Themes
The power of God; the miracles of Jesus;
resurrection and new life; bereavement and hope

Cast
Narrator
Martha
Mary
Lazarus
Jesus

Narrator	Once upon time there was Lazarus.
	A man who had two sisters.
	They were called Martha and Mary
	And they lived in a place called Bethany.
Martha	My name's Martha and I've lots to do
	I've got to cook the food and clean the loo.
(*She mimes cleaning.*)	
Mary	My name's Mary I like to listen and think.
	I like to watch Martha at the kitchen sink.
(*She looks relaxed and watches Martha.*)	
Martha	There's no time for that, there's no time to shirk
	Jesus is coming so we'd better get to work.

Narrator	Jesus was a very good friend
	And he often came round to visit them.
Lazarus	Oh dear I don't feel too well.
Martha	There's no time for that, there's no time to shirk
	Jesus is coming so we'd better get to work.
Lazarus	Oh dear I really don't feel too well.

(*Lazarus wanders off stage.*)

Martha	There's no time for that, there's no time to . . . Oh!

(*She sees he has gone.*)

Narrator	So they put him to bed, hoping he'd get better.
	Then lunchtime came round two hours later.
Martha	(*Calling off stage*) Lazarus, I've made you some of that soup you like.
	You'll soon be zooming round like a motorbike.
	Lazarus? Lazarus? Lazarus? Oh no.

(*Mary and Martha look off stage. They freeze.*)

Narrator	When Jesus arrived they were terribly sad.
	They'd lost the only brother they ever had.

(*Jesus walks on from the other side. They turn, see him and walk around him saying:*)

Mary and Martha	If only you'd come quicker
	You could have made him better.
	If only you'd come quicker
	You could have made him better.
	If only you'd come quicker
	You could have made him better.

(*They all embrace each other and sob silently.*)

Narrator	Jesus and Mary and Martha all cried for Lazarus, for they had lost a good friend.

> Then Jesus wiped his eyes, stood up, and did something which surprised all of them.

Jesus	Open the grave.
Mary and Martha	What?
Jesus	Open the grave.
Mary and Martha	What?
Jesus	Open the grave. And let him out!
	Open the grave.
Mary and Martha	What?
Jesus	Open the grave.
Mary and Martha	What?
Jesus	Open the grave. And let him out!
Narrator	They had put Lazarus in a very big cave.
	And rolled a stone in front to seal up the grave.
Jesus	Move the stone.
Narrator	With a push,
All	(*Miming pushing.*) Push!
Narrator	And a shove,
All	Shove! (*Miming shoving.*)
Narrator	And a big heave ho.
All	Heave – ho! (*Miming heaving.*)
Narrator	They opened up the grave and moved away the stone.
	Then Mary had a rest and Jesus gave a shout
	And Lazarus came walking out!

(*Mary and Martha lean back to back looking tired. Lazarus walks on stage wearing a blindfold. Mary and Martha leap in the air with fright and stare at him.*)

Narrator	They took off the blindfold and Lazarus could see
	They welcomed him back and Martha got some tea.

(*All freeze.*)

Ruth and Naomi

Bible references
Ruth 1

Themes
Friendship, devotion, loyalty, families

Cast
Narrator 1

Narrator 2

Ruth

Naomi (*Ruth's mother-in-law*)

Begin with the two narrators standing either side of the stage.

Narrator 1   What is friendship like?

Narrator 2   It's fun!

Narrator 1   Yes, sometimes. What else?

Narrator 2   Er . . . (*Thinks*) More fun!

Narrator 1   Yes, but what else?

Narrator 2   (*Thinks*) Er . . . Nice. And fun! Lots of fun. Always fun!

Narrator 1   Always?

Narrator 2   Yes. Always.

Narrator 1   Well, let's see. Let's have a look at this story.

Narrator 2   What? The one on this script? (*Holds up the script and points to it for all to see.*)

Narrator 1   Yes. That's the one. It's about Ruth and Naomi. Two very good friends.

Narrator 2   I bet it's a lot of fun then.

Narrator 1   Let's see shall we. It starts with Naomi. She's packed her case and is about to go on a long journey. Ruth's packing too.

(*Ruth walks on, carrying a case. She opens it and starts sorting out the clothes inside it. Then Naomi walks on. She is about to leave and is holding her own suitcase.*)

Naomi   Now Ruth I've got to go. I've packed everything and I am going home to the place where I was born. There's nothing here for me anymore. But there's plenty for you – you must stay here.

Ruth   No! I want to come with you to help you. There will be lots of things I can help you with.

(*Naomi takes the pile of clothes out of Ruth's case.*)

Naomi   You can't come.

(*Ruth puts them back in.*)

Ruth   Yes I can!

(*Naomi takes the pile of clothes out of Ruth's case.*)

Naomi   No you can't.

(*Ruth puts them back in.*)

Ruth   Yes I can!

(*Naomi takes the pile of clothes out of Ruth's case.*)

Naomi   Can't.

(*Ruth puts them back in.*)

Ruth   Can.

(*Naomi takes the pile of clothes out of Ruth's case.*)

Naomi   Can't.

(*Ruth puts them back in.*)

Ruth   Can.

(*Naomi takes the pile of clothes out of Ruth's case.*)

Naomi   Can't.

(*Ruth puts them back in.*)

Ruth	Can!

(*Narrator 1 holds up his hand and they freeze in mid action.*)

Narrator 1	This could go on all day. Let's cut to the chase . . .
Naomi	But your life is here. Your work is here. Your home is here. Your future's here.
Ruth	You're right.

(*Naomi kisses her and walks away.*)

Ruth	But I still want to come with you. I want to help you.

(*She runs after Naomi.*)

Naomi	But it's a long journey ahead. We'll get tired. It may be very wet and muddy.

(*She takes Ruth back to centre stage.*)

Ruth	Yes, you're right, it will be messy.

(*Naomi kisses her again and walks away.*)

Ruth	But I'm still coming.

(*She runs after Naomi.*)

Naomi	Is there anything I can say which will make you stay here?
Ruth	Yes.
Naomi	What? What can I say?
Ruth	Say you're not going.
Naomi	I can't. I am going. I came here a long time ago, when I had a big family. But now they've all gone, so I'm going back home. On my own.
Ruth	Then I'm coming too.
Naomi	It might be difficult.
Ruth	We'll help each other.
Naomi	It might be frightening.
Ruth	I'll try and be brave.
Naomi	You might not like it where we're going.

Ruth	No – but I'll pretend I do.
Naomi	I might get ill.
Ruth	I'll look after you.
Naomi	I might get lost.
Ruth	I'll bring a map. Wherever you go I will go. Wherever you want to live I will live. I'll always be your friend.
Naomi	Always?
Ruth	Always.

(They both give each other a hug and then freeze, still embracing. They hold this picture as the narrators finish their conversation.)

Narrator 1	See? Sometimes it's not easy to be a friend. But Ruth stuck by Naomi, even though it wasn't a lot of fun.
Narrator 2	What! You mean there was no fun at all?
Narrator 1	Oh yes.
Narrator 2	Thank goodness for that!
Narrator 1	Yes. Later on there was. Ruth and Naomi went back to Naomi's home and Ruth looked after Naomi. And before too long Ruth met a lovely, kind, wonderful man – and they got married. And then life was really good for them all again. And then they did have a lot of fun. The end.
Narrator 2	That's my bit.
Narrator 1	Is it? Oh, sorry.
Narrator 2	That's okay, I forgive you, you're my friend. *(To the audience)* Ladies and gentlemen – the end.

(The two narrators bow and leave. Ruth and Naomi stay frozen on stage. Narrator 2 then walks back on and whispers loudly to them from the side:)

Narrator 2	Pssst! Ruth! Naomi! Psst! That's the end!

(Ruth and Naomi turn and tip toe off stage. Narrator 2 looks at the audience, waves and leaves hurriedly.)

Other best-selling drama collections from

NATIONAL SOCIETY/CHURCH HOUSE PUBLISHING

Acting up
Dave Hopwood

Even more drama material by
Dave Hopwood.
£5.95

Sketches from Scripture
Derek Haylock

Another collection of lively sketches
designed to be performed with a
minimum of rehersal.
£5.95

Plays on the Word
Derek Haylock

Nineteen fast-moving, Bible-based
sketches, including eight for
Christmas.
£5.95

Plays for all Seasons
Derek Haylock

A collection of 21 dramas and plays
covering the whole Christian year.
£6.95

A Fistful of Sketches
Dave Hopwood

A wealth of sketches by the
ever-popular Dave Hopwood.
£5.95

All titles above are available from your local christian bookshop.

The National Society (Church of England) for Promoting Religious Education
supports everyone involved in Christian education – teachers, school governors,
students, parents, clergy, parish and diocesan education teams – with its legal and
professional advice, the resources of its RE centres, courses, conferences and archives.

It is a voluntary Anglican society, it also operates ecumenically, and helps to
promote inter-faith education and dialogue through its RE centres.

For more details of the Society or a copy of our current resources catalogue
and how you can support the continuing work of the Society,
please call or email: info@natsoc.org.uk